A Five
Year Journey

JD DeHart

A Five Year Journey
Copyright © 2018 by JD DeHart

Cover Art & Design:
Kristi King-Morgan
Cover Photograph:
Dre Graham
Editor:
Larissa Banitt
Interior Formatting:
Niki Browning
Editor-in-Chief:
Kristi King-Morgan

Printed in the United States of America

First Printing, 2018

ISBN-13: 978-1-947381-10-0
ISBN-10: 1-947381-10-5

Dreaming Big Publications

www.dreamingbigpublications.com

TABLE OF CONTENTS

INTRODUCTION

In 2012, I was teaching English and writing scraps here and there when I felt somewhat inspired. Before that, I usually threw first drafts away and never bothered to share or submit many.

My first dabble into writing was in the 1990s, with a "Writer's Market" and an arsenal of stamps and envelopes at my disposal. I had a few successes, but the process was long and I was still honing my skills. In the early 2000s, I went on a sort of unofficial creative hiatus. Today, I'm still not sure why.

My family always encouraged me to write, and my wife suggested that I begin writing again. She has always been a supporter of my work, and has helped me become a better writer. So, I began submitting more. I made use of new tools and new spaces to expand my writing. I also made use of what I had learned over the years to improve my work.

This is the second collection of poetry I have put together. The first, "The Truth About Snails," was written during a break from my classroom work and mostly consisted of poems inspired by science fiction. It was published in 2014 by Red Dashboard.

"A Five Year Journey" is, in many ways, a more personal collection. There are a few poems here that have been featured around the web and in various publications over the years, but the majority of these poems are new. They contain reflections on beliefs, teaching, and writing, as well as notes on life in general.

I am continuing my journey as a writer, and I hope you enjoy reading what I have gathered here.

A FIVE-YEAR JOURNEY

"Put your words out there,"
she said to me, my inspiration,
the one who has encouraged me
all this while, "go on and send your
verbs out into the wind.
            see which ones float back,
                which ones take off to the stars."

"Put your words into the world,
son," my parents told me.
So I added them up, I took account
of the many journeys my mind
tried to make, stamped them,
and there they went.

I recalled long walks in the woods,
hikes with my dad,
all the stories and plots and details
collected over time,

and five years ago started deleting
less and sending more, sharing, trying,
prodding. What stands now
is what will hopefully be the first stone
on which many more will be piled,
just pushing around pebbles with my nose.

PATH ALL GROWN

There are bears here now,
and coyote. Which brings to mind
the story of the wolves following
the creek bed.

Gun powder and blast sound
spreading in the air did not
send them fleeing. Refusing
to leave, they stood their ground.

That is why I have not walked
on the path in years, so well-trod
with my father when I was young,
now grown up, covered with brambles.

Travel now would take some time
anyway, hesitations and stops,
as we clear away what chokes.

REBUTTAL

A flat slam of door
sums up the argument, but
an argument it has not been.
More letting go, an oblation.

More like a lamentation
about all the ills and wrongs,
each adversity wind born.
A shower of winds for lack
of delight.

When I part my lips to
respond, having rolled my rebuttal
into a dung-beetle ball,

Off you go, refusing to listen,
comfortable with your own catharsis,
leaving me longing for closure.

Nevermind, I will direct my comments
to these matryoshka dolls lined up,
each one opening with a new word
only to close on the same one.

SAILING

The slap of water is somewhere
to the right. Somewhere on the darkened
surface is a small vessel.

It could be seen moments ago, but now the moon
is obscured. A bridge, in the distance,
rises and falls as cars blink across like
eyelids. The sound of tiny crabs clattering
against each other is somewhere below.

Inside the old structure, overlooking
the water, settlers and workers carved
words and ideas that no longer make sense.

Like two hundred years from now if someone
reads this poem, their then-language unlike
mine, trying to make sense of where the boat
may really be.

Right Hand Man

It is probably too late to say
this, but be careful of the circular
saw in December. It ends badly.

Warnings are not as useful
now since we do not have the power
to travel back. Maybe one day.
I wish I could help now.

The story itself is one of horror,
makeshift bandage, quick one-handed
travel to the hospital. Stuttering orders.

All this while the rest of the world
caught a film, had a light flaky seafood
dish for dinner, unwrapped gifts.
Unaware of trouble, just a few miles away.

This Process

All of these spinning wheels,
churning agendas, this scent of stinging
smoke that lingers in the air, unseen,
conjures images of the chute systems
cows must navigate in order to be
led to the slaughter. My goodness.

That may seem a bit bleak, but think
of the majesty of a mass-produced
system, the Gesellschaft gears
ensuring there is a blueprint for everything,
complete with kinks, bumps, uncertainties,
even blind corners.

Road maps are few and far between.
The students sit in rows waiting
for a test that will place them on longitudinal
paths for life; the assessment is riddled with
issues, and issues with riddles.

Sharpen your pencils, turn to page one.

Root Bound

Reach, yearn, stretch.
That's it, think yoga. Downward-
facing dog.

This is a morning of new growth,
opportunity. Practice
being fecund with possibility,
verdant with positivity.

An open door waits at either side
of the residence. Walk through,
take a powerful protein lunch.
You're gonna need it.

Clear the throat of all detritus.

Today is the day that the attire
of business delivers a smug greeting,
everyone forgets we are just creatures
playing a game here with spreadsheets,
insurance policies, stacks of paper
that have been assigned arbitrary values.

A hierarchy, someone else's hegemony,
is buried, deep rhizome workings.

Yesterday I attempted to pull what
I thought was a weed, but was instead

pleasant mint, the many reaching fingers
of the plant's root signaling, *Step away,*

I am just trying to spread here.
I am working on my 401k.

THE FRANKENSTEIN WORD GAME

Curious how a word clings
to a word, a string of words making
a sentence. Samuel Johnson said
that language is the dress of thought.

When we are quiet, should we feel
a sense of social nudity?

Should those that are loquacious feel
as if they are burdened with extra
garment layers?

Someone else once said that "ain't"
ain't a word. But an utterance communicating
meaning is, by definition, a word.
Unless the definition has changed.

Dusty dictionaries have been long time
companions. Rewriting their sentences was an
occasional punishment. Knowledge
of the schwa and its meaning, representation,
give a sense of having read them.

Curious how a simple word can be taken,
features added like fragments of other beings,
gathered in the advantage of a restless midnight.
One never knows where lightning might

strike, or where the composed word signals
an abrupt ending to the story.

AVENUE OF THE SEA

Like some ancient figure out
of a strange story, the sea was parted
for our path.

A quivering, fish-flopping world
of creatures out of their comfort
zones, suddenly revealed to us.

A bird reaches down to embrace
one of the ocean creatures, but the kiss
is characteristically violent.

Now a parting of narrative, a turning
of proverbial page, because one day
this path will find caesura.

The sea will resume its natural ellipsis,
we will again be on dry land, reminding
ourselves to be changed by the travel.

Dignitary

When you arrived, the three dignitaries
had already been seated,
each wearing yellow, giving
one another knowing smiles,
dressed like round suns.

Imagine your surprise when
you looked down and realized
you too were dressed in yellow,
the strange dynamic of difference
when you realized for a moment
you might have a voice.

The words of a pedagogue came
rushing back: Get smart. What will
you do with a position of power?

Until opportunity was snuffed away by
insecurity or the need of another
to chew the air with fierce words,
never affording you the chance to speak.

ORATOR

A modicum of academic
throat-clearing. Standing
falsely profound at the podium.
A dance of words and citations,
throwing names and dates
into the air, and the unfortunate
truth that most of these findings
were lost somewhere in translation
between the second and third row.
An audience that stops listening
after fifteen minutes in an hour-
long presentation, the back row
lulling themselves to slumber
by counting the reference list.

THE SNAIL RETURNS

Yes, it's been a while, old friend.
I feel as if I can hardly call you that.
How I admire your shell, even as you
cling to the side of the porch, even as
I engage in the sweaty work of an 89
degree afternoon. Even as you laugh
and jeer inside the coil of your spiraling
shell. Your color is cream in places,
like cloying candies from my youth;
in other spots, you are burnt sienna,
like the dog's shit on the front lawn.
I really must find a way to dispatch
that dog. But you can stay, even
though we both know what you are
thinking, waving oracular eyebrows
at me. we both remember the dish
of beer I left out for you to sink into,
but, certainly, stay for just right now.

NOW DON'T YOU KNOW

Gathered around their microwavable
meals, I learned so much about how
not to be. Listening to their banter,
sometimes light with buttery bathroom
jokes, other times heavy with dramatic
rumor. I heard and forgot more about
sports that one season than I ever care
to again. Now, don't you know
they had an affair in the 1990s. Really?
I struggle with the pairing of images
this accusation entails. Oh, yes, really.
Would I lie? Then the day I found out
that everyone at the table was a liar,
discovering how their stories would
begin as a rib bone, then be a full-fledged
screaming hormonal teenager by afternoon.
It was not long before I began
travelling away in my mind, imagining
them as apes or vultures leaning over
a carcass in the judgmental sun.

COUGH

That art of covering your mouth,
where has it gone? As I watch the film,
images flickering, inviting me to escape
a few brief moments in an hour, all I can
think is how bits of pathogen wave in
the closed air of this room. How each
sneeze and cough bears with it a few days
in bed, slunk low, sipping cough medicine
or fiery whiskey to clear the throat, doing
little for the senses. The space becomes
so clotted with reflections on the infirm
that the movie is over before I know it,
but I am still sitting, wondering how I
can open the door to leave, enter the day
again, gripping the door when I chose
to wear short sleeves again, in spite of the
inhospitable cold. How John
Donne's flea carried with it germs, promise,
and how I do not want the germs of these
many theatergoers fecund inside me.

CLARITY

In a dim Saturday night lightbulb
he saw himself for one moment
in time as he truly was,

as if not just catching
a reflection
but being in a closed-frame,
a supernatural still-life.

In that moment,
the question: Do I like
what I see, have I ever liked
this person?

There is no shock to the answer,
no climactic surprise,
as he mills about,

turning over vegetables
to look for rotten spots
that are not there.

BALL PLAYERS

A rumble of voices
talks about the game. I don't
understand this game, but at
least there is passion in the play
by play.

I've watched from the stands
maybe ten times. Much movement,
loud sounds. Wondering what
happens if the ball comes too close.
Thinking about after the game.

My afternoons now punctuated
by the sounds of neighborhood
ballplayers. Maybe playing the way
I would have if I had tapped into
athletic culture as a child. Ignited
by the thump of a ball on pavement,
a small object flying through the air.

No, I just don't see it.

GRAVEDIGGER

There must have been
the sound of thunder the day
my dad served as pallbearer.
A signal of the rain.

I heard about the slick
earth, how hard the digging
was, but only appreciated

such challenge after traipsing
through packs of snow, listening
to a graveside sermon about
cattle going mad from an unseasoned
parson doing his best,
a strange reference not connected
to the person in earth's crib.

He carried the coffin, mud baptizing
a new pair of light brown shoes.

Severance Pay

Goodbye, the static in the air
spoke in a voice that was less than soft.
We won't be needing you here
anymore.

So, they sent him home to his family
whose saucer eyes saw him
coming through the door, what
did he have left to say?

A sign of failure started small
in the yard, in the back of the house,
spread throughout, upstairs, downstairs,
a Dickens novel ....

until one day the family was
there no more, just a vacancy
where names used to be.

ANALYZING ONE'S OWN POETRY

It is a snake reversing
trying to kiss itself, and we
know the kisses of snakes
can be tremendously awful.

Here is a line I wrote
when feeling out of touch
with the child I used to be.

Here is another when pining
for a lost love I never lost
but simply made up.

And who knows where this
one came from at all?

Pillow Origami

I'm sorry, I will never
be as skilled
at folding fabric as I should,
the movements elude me.

What you make is beautiful,
an artwork of thread woven
through thread, patchwork
that does not look like patchwork,
it looks like it was intended to be this way
from the start of heaven,

and is neatly folded for
maximum comfort.

I simply do not have this gift.
I can make a rough
pile of stitches, I can shove unused
pillow cases in a drawer,

but a seam ripper? Forget it.

BEHEADED SHEEP FIGURINE

The budding voices have died away,
Leaving the empty room with confetti
Spread on the rarely clean floor,
Small tokens of their presence.

In the middle of the room, beneath a table,
A plastic sheep, the head chewed off,
An abandoned Old Testament sacrifice.

JD DeHart

Pursuits

A small bit of leisure
at the end of a long road.

And what can I not find myself
embedded in the words of a harrowing
true story?

Perhaps it is all the words that
have already passed me by.

I must take a small breather, a swimmer
at the side of the pool, before
diving back in for a few more laps.

I must take lessons in how to take
lessons, must sign up, decide one day
the absolute direction.

Only then will my legs move
without becoming overly sore.

DRY LAND

It stretches out for the bare foot,
where all was water.

There is still evidence of
sea creatures.

They say the whole earth
used to be moving liquid
before a voice woke it.

I imagine storms all the time,
but maybe those eons were
calm.

I move from basin to basin,
not being a swimmer myself.
Wishing to sail, enjoying
the sense of salt in the air,

listening for a whisper from
heaven to call my name.

JOHN RAMM

When first domesticated, John was given
A power tie and a mug with antlers.
He was informed about corporate life
Now he paces in the offices
Snorting and bucking, attempting to climb.
The heights are sheer.
This is what his hooves are made for,
They talk about him at the water cooler.

We Caged the Minotaur

When we first found him,
he was so alive,
playing his little game
at the center of that
whatever it's called.

Now he just sits, listless,
with empty eyes. T-shirt
sales spiked two months
ago.

Since then, the interest
has waned. Nobody wants
to see a sad, moping, dull
creature of lore.

Pretty soon we'll ship him
off and he can spend his
final sad days in a sadder
zoo and all of us will have
moved on.

OPERATOR

My aunt Sheila was an operator.
In the old days, when you picked up,
Said "Operator" she would be
There, passing out advice.

She would manually unplug a wire,
Then plug it in another location
To establish connection.

There are stories of operators
Listening in on the affairs of politicians.
JFK comes to mind.

That plugging process, the physical
process of actual connection,
like plugging one life into another.
I wonder if she thought of names
When she tugged at the wires.

RAIN DELAY

Pardon me as I string
some sense together, I had no idea
we would have swum here.

I expected a day at home
reclining, and this is the problem
with last minute planning.

I wanted to move the earth
and change the world, but today, as rain
comes slapping down outside
this room with no windows,

I search for the right sounds,
try to arrange a few images
to send some meaning home,

but my message drowns in the swirl.

NABOKOVIAN

The first time I met Nabokov,
I only wanted to read him because
I knew "Lolita" was tawdry, a reason
Steeped in juvenile thought.
Quickly, I saw the poetic movement,
Finding his voice through transparent
Embers of verse, the confessions
Of an aging pedagogue, the Kafkaesque
Story of Cincinnatus, decapitated,
The Orwellian police state narrative,
All bearing witness to a writer
Adept, thoughtful, yet learning English
As a language second to Russian.

REQUIEM FOR A NEIGHBOR

I never would have learned to double-lace
If not for him, and would still have strapping
Sounds of my shoe strings hitting sidewalks.

The children in the yard call Marco,
No one is there to reciprocate. Even if they
Were to call from rooftops, no roosters
Would be around to crow in response.

How did he die? What can we say?
It was an asteroid, we want to lie, but in truth
He was a victim of peristalsis, the less
Said, the better for his headstone dignity.

So, yes, we will stick with the space story,
The victim of a random shooting star.

HARDSCRABBLE

The field caught fire
in a spark of natural vengeance.
Maybe a cigarette, or
a spark from nowhere?

What pain was known before
I knew that place?
They carried buckets of water
as fast as they could.

Closed walls, a journal expressing
in lightest ink the feeling of being
trapped. A sensation below
the surface, unseen like some marine
animal, ready to surface.

The surface came finally
when the house woke and a familiar
voice wasn't there, a speech empty
in the air where life used to be.

Favorable Conditions

The ground was filled with
static, sky pregnant with bruising
rage, when the downpour started.

It was a perpetual build-up,
stone upon stone, over decades.
Before I even knew it.

For my part, I had had enough.
Listening to the complaints weigh down
clouds, foul words about decent people.

Voices like axes trying to chop down
trees, an hour or two a day.
Full of venomous, negative dirge.

So, it was what might be called
a perfect storm, a furious laughter leaving
my mouth as I left that space.

Ashland, North Carolina

Place of breathing pipes,
blinking lights of many colors,
speaking into the nighttime.

We drove through on our way
to some outdoor festival, late
at night, thumping music.

Did I stay awake the whole time?
It seems so. The taste of iced coffee
with nothing else to flavor it.
Passage through the ravaged earth

brief though it was, has stuck,
a pinned note in my memory,
that mechanical world glimpsed,
factory sounds in lyrical pauses.

POSITION

I have been
written into position, hedged
by words and experience.

Are they a hedge, a boundary,
or a boost? It's hard to tell
from here. So close to the earth.

A series of isms and regions
embodied in a few phrases,
I could break free, but who needs
to break free? I would have to adopt
an itchy persona, in any case.

Accepting the position
a word makes, a dialect offers,
I establish without embellishing,
recognizing the politics of space.

Admitting it is all political.

DINER MUSE

She's got the swivel
joints of a worker bee,
spinning like a gear. How
does she balance those trays?

Not trying to be sexist here;
goodness knows, I'd spill those
plates all over the floor.
Angry patrons, a pink slip,
inevitable.

Each plate weighs as much as any
heavy judgment, and there are
at least five on each dais.

Umbrella

Above, a layer
of thin veneer protects
from the onslaught. It's
been too long since we had
rain, after all. Pollen,
the scent of October smoke,
washed away in gushing bouts
down the streetway.
Emptied into some unseen
chasm, the hiding place of all the griefs
of half a year.
How that skin stretched between
thin metal bones offers safe passage.
How I might offer to extend
its yawn to another passerby.

JD DeHart

PRONE

Spread out
the filet of a fish
smiling up at the wide
open universe.

The mind tries
to tether stars
and unseen celestial
objects to
no avail.

We cannot contain the world
even as we are of it,
born of its earth,
breathing its air, and slurping
its waters.

We do what we can in
our brief blink of a while.

BRITISH ACCENT

Go on, try it on,
a bit of British accent.

When you go a new school
try it out, see what others will
do, how they will respect you for your
new accent.

While you're at it, try coming up with
a cheery nickname.

Try to hold it up, that accent,
practice it often, don't let it get shaky,
slipping in and out.

Of course, this is all probably ill-advised,
but there is freedom in finding who
you are in a brand-new location.

JD DeHart

Lensing

Let the camera flare,
this is the way the image
is represented. Turning the device
on its head,
the room appears in a fuzzy
convolution on the screen

      then, how am I seen?

I wave awkwardly, my arm
appearing to move in a way
I did not expect, thinking:
Is this what I look like all the time
when I wave? Moving
like a tin man,

my portrait soon flickering to
someone else's, now thinking:

Do they have the same perception
of themselves, a sudden,
humbling surprise? Or do they think,
here is my beauty, cast on the wall?

ENTRENCHED

Buried deep
in an office, just borrowing
space. Conjuring

memories of ticks from the forest
of growing up, tiny creatures
that would hitch rides
then snuggle too closely
with the skin,

recasting the connotation
of entrenchment for myself.
No longer pest or pathogen-
spreading louse,

but given a place
so that the world cannot be moved
but maybe adjusted, if only a little.

RAPT

Holding the mind
as in vise
      (not an easy task)
a bit of engagement will do
      (edutainment)
mixing the metaphor, sound
bright blinking picture,
      but,
here in the real world,
I can hardly change the camera
angle,
      the blinking must be up
      to you.
      (So)
      involve your perception,
get a grab-hold somewhere,
wherever you can,
before I am gone sipping
a latte
and the big test comes.

SEMESTER'S END

They say his boxes
were all packed, the door shut
as he left the last time.
Lesson done.

I remember his gentle manner,
how easily he could have eviscerated
all the students in the room
with the subtle turning of a word,
this man with two doctoral degrees.

But his learning was a kind one,
the brand of matriculation I want to offer,
not the harsh speech that sends
a student out in tears, considering, flustered.

To spread incision with verbiage
is not to be intelligent.

SAND CASTLE

How the Bible gives us
one side, then the other;
it is as if God is saying to us,
"Work it out, people, talk about it,
love each other and figure together."

But we are so much better
at divisions, hurrying to boundaries,
children protecting our corners,
our tiny sand castles, huddling
in greedy circles.
Meanwhile, the Father is whispering:
"The tide is coming, it does not matter,
this castle will crumble anyway,
stop clinging to sand."

CUSTODIAN TO THE YOUNG

A kid refuses to look at the book,
as if reading the words might give him
late stage leprosy, while
his neighbor
unstitches a baseball to pass the time.
There is a quiet competition going on
somewhere in the room involving
knuckles and quarters.
They all wear faces
that are not quite
their own, smiling at the teacher
one of those put-up-with-you grins,
spouting political opinions overheard
from their parents in other rooms.
Statistics say at least three
of them
have suffered some abuse,
maybe even this morning
before class.
Children move in their own circles.
They try all the doors for locks and levels,
reaching out to find buttons to push
like a dashboard of dainty delights.
"I hate Obama," one says.
 "I do too," another replies.
Neither knowing why, or how,
or what it really means.
A third chimes in,

"Why do I have to learn to read anyway?
None of this matters to me, it's so stupid."
Teacher stands with book held up, refusing
to let the pages curl up and crisp completely,
reciting again the bold Jimenez quote.

Narrative Creature

Born of story
built together, sinew
to sinew, word by word,

page by page, stepping
and stomping, becoming,
until given a name.

Then scratched out
and tossed into
a wastepaper basket.

JOHN RAMM'S RETIREMENT PARTY

This poem is for the recently departed
Mr. John Ramm, a dedicated co-worker
who was found one day grazing in a field,

and who now exists in the halls of this
great company's memory. A horned figure
once stuffed into a business suit, now
mounted upon the wide victory wall.

Symbolism Takes a Seat

In walked dear symbolism,
whom I invited so often to
class with me, and down
she sat.
Along the ride, she pointed
out the plumage of bright
birds flapping past, perhaps
resembling courage;
a pool standing stagnant
representing my lack;
an old man signaling
the inevitability of my fall.
Dear, you read too deeply,
she told me as she left,
just enjoy the rest of the trip,
which I took to mean life.
But maybe not.

A History of Bad Ideas

Here is a history of bad ideas
horribly woven together.

The narrative of truth bubbles below
the surface. Listen.
There is always another side to the coin,
always another story to be told.

Listen to the whisper of history from
stones, if you like,
the wail of history from street corners.

Each moment a slight reminder
of something that passed before,
but do we note it and then remember?

COMPOSURE

Broken static, crisp the sound
of a cord snapping.
Undulations of a pool moments
ago serene, now whispering
swish sounds of demise.
Swinging electric set, sparks
decorating the atmosphere,
spilling down on to the sidewalk.
Bits of firelight like insects
showing dark corners of the yard
at night: jagged fingers that are
blades of grass, slithering animals
that are garden gloves and mislaid
toys. Given venom without light,
infused with unprecedented force.
This is the nature of the temper
when aroused, the inferno of talk
unfettered by formal conversation.
The breaking point of many years,
a verbal living room conflagration.

BLACKBALL

Marvel at how the dung
beetle makes a tiny mark
on the universe, rolling its
excess into a heap.
How thoughtful of the beetle.
If only we could be like
that insect, cognizant of the ways
we use our own waste, aware
of how much we carry it with us.
I am not talking about simple
recycling here; this is an emotional
discussion. Take, for instance,
all the fears that have held me
back these many years. Roll
them, blackball them quite literally,
toss them in a corner, make them
stand up in a Jane Eyre chair, and
toss taunts their way for a change.
Now that would-be Mother Nature's
handiwork at its finest, a knife's
tip balance of surging irony.

LOPSIDED

Balance can take on so
many meanings, so many applications.
The ballerina who miraculously
places her entire being onto the small
space provided by two toes,
holding up ontology with a few
bits of bone and muscle.
A political conversation, poised
on the cusp of finger-pointing,
amazingly traversed with only
modest amounts of torment.
A whispering cacophony of a room
full of little learners, children chained
to desks, pencils raised, ready to begin
what is sure to be the test that will
decide some important life factor,
show the way to some future path,
or simply be crumpled up, a bad copy,
thrown into the trash. An akimbo
exercise following a balanced diet
or reading, arithmetic, and rules.
Someone's plans and goals in pencil-
thin lead markings, heavy erasure.

A Balm of Words

If words
could offer a balm
like the leaves of rare,
exotic plants, the smooth
slathering of aloe, threatening
an almost frigid presence,
bringing a sudden ecstasy
of moisture to sun-burnished skin,
then I would offer a word,
at least one.

If voice could restore
faith and confidence, then
I would have been filled
in the rumbling car, shielded
from summer, winter, even
the seasons of my inner life.

I would have been built,
constructed, in the space
of a vehicle, shaped in transit,
arriving complete, packaged,
instant human being, add
a modicum of praise.

Spinning Out

Feeling the need for control,
challenged by the moment.
A tire rises, like a dove
above the earth,
far from arks and promises,

when rain
pounds so vigorously no one
can see the road, or else
the world goes into a topsy-
turvey delusion, waiting to
be righted, waiting, dizzy,

> I know there was
> a road here,
> where did it go?

A decided lack of power.

MUST BE REAL

This moment must be real,
a grizzly bear pretending
to be a human says, "No
need to even pinch, I bite,
of course."

He describes how he wakes
with a sore on the inside
of his cheek from chewing
over his stresses in the night.

I realize for maybe the first time
the forest is not a place of calm.

How he cannot sleep Sunday
nights because Monday is coming,
uncertain of what to do, or how
he is doing any of it.

> What if fish stop
> appearing in the stream?

It's all certainly real, unless
he is simply a manifestation
of a modern human condition,
of a modern human condition,
an allegory lumbering out of a Kafka
novel with a short title.

MASTER OF DISGUISE

I am not master of disguise,
the pulp paperback trench coat
has no place here. I wouldn't
know what to do with a detective's
hat if I had an entire warehouse full.

Not the mustache of indifference,
the long flowing gown of uncertainty,
nor the camouflage of now you see me,
now where am I....

I am not a lump of clay to be molded,

embracing my own Appalachian
enclitic, the sound of my raising, cadence
of speech, the who I am and where I am
headed, the hay fever seasons

and all else be damned,
no great mysteries to solve here.

JD DeHart

It Will Be Okay, You'll See

No longer the one
who soaks in the bath of confidence-
building, I offer a solid word,
a sudsy warm pool of consolation,
block of stone verbiage:

Your ankle will not slip
again from the pavement, sending
you spiraling, no, not so long as I am
here to be a shoulder, or even a finger.

Even if you should pull me down
with you, I will do my best to provide
a soft landing, no elbows rising
to greet you like a violent lyric.

No longer a by-word, no longer
a curse, a path full of blessing, because
it really will be fine. You'll see.
Really, now, after all.

PLAY ON WORDS

A verb came for a visit,
blowing into the front yard,
all intensity.
The many little children came out
to offer greeting.

I had no idea kids were so plentiful,
existing in our neighborhood,
roaming onto the lawn like a band
of feral cats.

Soon enough, a noun, then an
adjective. All the other trappings
of junior high grammar class, enough
for full-on play, then falling into
an afternoon nap, reclining on
parts of language for a light slumber.

Every sentence, a soft cot.

ODDS ON

It's rattle
a cage kind of melody
punctuated by minimal
breaks in sound
like the animal musings
of capture.

"Don't worry," someone
tells the man with thick
fingers, "everyone has
these bad days when the chips
don't fall like they should."

But it's been a long season
of chips falling strangely:

lumps under the skin, bad
prognoses, multiple procedures,
the glint of a metal brace,
shattered windshields.

He tries to respond with all
this, but only the rattle again,
somewhere deep in the back of
his throat, a shadow swallowed
by a whale.

I Wrap You in Metaphor

I would wrap
you in the gossamer
bed of a honey bee's
necessary work, taking away
the sting, maintaining honey,
wrap you in the collection
of words that found
a reader, for you deserve
to be taken in, cared for,
noticed by someone.
I would wrap up our past
days in ruthless perfection,
wash out the many sins
I've scattered on our path,
sharp little shard breadcrumbs,
wipe away misplaced words,
leaving a perfect, wondrous
metaphor, but I stumble
when I get to
        it's kind of like.

JD DeHart

Bird or Beast

A nest always exists,
it comes back every year.
There's no avoiding it.

The first year, we nursed
the eggs but they must
have been stolen by a cat.
One day, they simply
weren't.

After that, we mourned,
but there was another nest.
These hatched, but a storm
passed through, tossing bare,
tender bodies onto the cold
boards.

Now the nests are higher,
we check them as best we can
from the earth's mooring,
clinging to hope of life.

CAUGHT

An old man goes up
and down the street,
casting his lure onto
the pavement, the rod
and reel angling
back and forth.

It's like muscle memory
or a nostalgic form
of motion contemplation.

He smiles at me when I
ask if he has caught
anything yet.

HERE IS A SIMPLE TEST

you can administer any time you like.
Just add water, then vinegar.
Drop in a dash of pepper.
Now measure your sense of growing
impending doom.
Now compare that to a friend.
Ask them how they feel about the end
of the world. Are they making plans?
Have they written anything down?
Some cultures don't. It's like putting
your head in the sand. It's like pretending
you don't have a head, that there is no
sand, that sand is not a thing.
Sand is a thing. I have seen it. I pick it out
of my clothing at the beach.
The beach is also a thing. Here is a simple
test. See how many people you trust.
Is that number dwindling? Welcome to the
club, baby girl.

AN EVENING IN THE COUNTRY

Whining music like a warbling
voice comes streaming up from
the hollow.

We are gathered around
a pan, shelling beans, listening
to the metallic ping of sound.

A tree stands above us, the one
the white cat ran up to escape
the pack of dogs that raved through.

One day the tree will fall, but not
today, not even this decade.

GRAMMAR RULES

Listen
to the sound of the language
telling you its inner rhythm.

Of course, if all else fails
you could try exercises 136-139,
copy some pages.

My hand still hurts and my
mind is still bleary
with my own grammar book
experiences;

rather than swiftly
navigating the surface of a sentence
we drill through it,
hollowing out the core.

GUTTER MYSTERY

The absence of image
from one panel to the next
leaves it to me to fill
the void (a second, a moment,
an eternity)? Realizing the gap
between image and image,
I fill in the details on my own,
reminding myself of the features

not completely filled in.

JD DeHart

FLICKERS

Pardon me for attempting to interrupt
an otherwise heroic show.
These lines have long been rehearsed.
The reshoots ridiculous.

I know my mistake in a cinematic
instant. The flicking projector
tongue pronounces my error.

Pardon the ghoulish words
and the shattered costume,
all of this should be a lavish set design.
I'm improvising here.

Taking my exit stage left or right
or whatever is closer, I say,
"enjoy the rest of the show."

Others are far more polished than I am.

Always Redemption

The message
always rebirth, arriving
on the wind or on the spine
of the just-right sentence.

We are not content
as we are
always pressing forward, always
changing,

letting our nature be turned
as we go, collecting experience
and (hopefully) wisdom as we
sip our daily cups.

> The hero moves into the climax
> of the story, the greatest battle
> of the character's life, only
> to be changed in a way that moves
> the narrative forward.

JD DeHart

Tell the Story

Write your story
in pen or ink, or whatever
you can find that makes
a mark.

Sketch your story
on the back of a sheet of paper
or the lonely wall

in small marks
where you can,
in large marks
where everyone can see.

Declare your name
and what life has taught you
asking yourself:

What is the story inside of my life
that will not be quiet?

CONCRETE SENTENCE

Three-foot cord
with a slab of stone in the middle
of July heat.

This is the sentence.

I would go and set you free
creature
if I could, the unkindness of people
stitched across your bones.

The ramshackle
home forming a base for your pining
inside, maybe a shadow,
a flicker of television,

someone who does not deserve
another creature.

JD DeHart

Red Dog in the Sun

We offered
food, but kindness was mistaken
for malice.

The small figure trotted off
as best it could with stark
form,

wasted words trailing behind
as it passed the Do Not Trespass
sign that warded us off.

SOMNAMBULANT

Forget the rush and rust
of creaking metal rolling down the highway
at super-speed, set aside all thoughts
of what happens when an engine explodes,

embrace the feeling of a carpeted floor
on your bare feet in the night.
In that moment when it is only you
observing the silent world outside.

All the others are still asleep with the modest
exception of you; a persistent barking dog,
miles away but still heard; and the one or two
people you know who work nightshifts,

populating this time with their action,
still and far away while the rest of the world
spins, spirals, and searches, these nocturnal
dwellers welcome your voice.

JD DeHart

FEATHER PERCUSSION

From a distant puce field, full of grain
not only waving but practically screaming
invitation, our rustle-walking unsettled
the flock enough for it to beat the air with its
mottled wings, interrupted only by a
sudden cacophonous shotgun sound,
impossible to tell if it came from my father's
gun, or a rival woodsman, invisible to us.

Then the song is over.

DENSITY

There is a mysterious weight to the air.
We cannot achieve warmth, we cannot
find a cool temperature, balanced on a flu-
like fever sense, missing homeostasis.

One day I will join the earth, either
by wooden vessel or in a flash of ash, or
else I will join the crackle of lightning above,
letting life by another definition scoop me
up. It's all a little hard to make sense of.

Sometimes the most clarity I find all
day, along with the most comfort, is in the first
few moments before light has shown through
the windows, when I think only about
concepts of like morning, my mind elsewhere.

GIVE THE HEART

A whisper? A shout
from heaven? Who knows how
best God decides to speak?
A bit of dots or syllables. The mystery
of a rolling cloud.

Give me the whole,
all the fears, this strange
fear of failure that summons,
that quakes,
let it go.

Give me the stomach
with all its hunger, the mind with
all its wandering, the center
down to the core.

Taking what I know
of myself and offering to what
I know of eternity.

GRAY STRANDS

Where full vibrancy
used to be, now there is a fleck
of gray.

And the flecks grow.
Soon, they will be full tides,
lapping waves of age
running over my brow.

A waterfall of withered
experience. But how soon is soon?
I know this day has come swiftly,
but I know time is relative.

My father's face looks back
at me in the window
that is really a mirror.

LECTURELY

This voice
barely fills the front of the room,
I know, I know,

I need a microphone, but
if you will just listen to a phrase
or two,

perhaps jot a note here
or there, maybe there will be a
kernel to share.

How many words have I spent
uselessly in a room full of people
who have no ears?

Hands whose bodies will not
let them write?

Frog

Threads in slime
or beautiful emerald
tapestry, an invitation
to sit on the lily pad.

A prince is only
in there if you believe
legends and fairy tales.

Otherwise, he's just
the bulbous eye, tadpole
producing, croaking bellow
that keeps you up nights.

POLAR

Icy,
his form flowing
from the cold
center of north.

How
we tried to thaw
him, but no
such luck.

When
he saw us
through foggy
breath, knowing us,
we recognized
the gleam
of isolation.

LEARNING HOW TO USE A SWORD

I used to have
a sword, but it was blunt
and disappointing.
I had no idea how to stand
with a blade. Then, one day
at a gun show, a man told me
people used to defend their
families in the Civil War
with these things. Now
I don't even bother to pick
one up, and that's the best
way sometimes, really,
to handle a sword.

GRANDFATHER

We installed rollers to make the movement simple.
Daily, we took notice of his toenails,
Their thickness or thinness, their shade.
We kept the results in a journal
While he told us stories of his youth.
The family nodded and read his diagnostics.

HEROES NEED FICTION

The strong warrior
reaches for his arrow,
but finds it removed
from his narrative.
The brave man thinks back
to page three to remind
himself of how he became
so brave. If only we had
our own stories to stand
on and remind ourselves
of why we decided
to become noble in the first
place, on the first page.

JD DeHart

THEM'S THE BREAKS

I remember
the story of the boy who wanted
to save the world.

Who visited the statue each
day, listening for the right words
he had never been taught.

It was all pissing in the dark, of course,
major guesswork,
like the theme of adulthood.

Feeling with our feet as we go
so we can break new ground,
trusting heaven that the earth beneath
will not fall.

MANDIBLE

Foraging, the insect tells
a story about creation. I picture
my own face decorated with
such a mandible, my own
physiognomy encased in a Kafka
carapace, grateful for miscellany.

DISSECTING THE CLOUD

Conversation goes beyond what
can easily be notated on a slip
of lined paper, debates about concepts
that hang in the air like bits of hail,
bobbing up and down in dance until
they are heavy enough to strike earth.
Motion like oil derricks, but far from
being crude instruments,
a description of the philosophical
and theological unseen, words dressed
with the same fury of any debate
upon the contents of precise beakers.

Representation

To take the word and conjure
it in mixed media, to take another's
narrative and wrap it in our own
metaphor, playing the game of placing
or noting emerging codes. To take
many paragraphs and truncate them
in a few verses, each word is a symbol,
oil swirl painting idea on canvas,
a representation of experience, complete
and yet incomplete, already here
and not yet arrived.

JD DeHart

A Jo Bell Poem

Yes, the family
was far-flung, the wounds
were made deep.

What he built
was decidedly razed,

he was the subject
of much celestial debate.

A whirlwind appeared
to him, inciting questions,
others could not answer,
so they went away.

IMAGE AND SOUND

A curious
combination of picture,
movement, gesture, sound.

Making a meaning.

A few scripted
words, echoing
in the mostly empty room,

met by a few chuckles,
the audience's muted reaction.

A floor littered with popcorn
and a few devoted fans
wishing for sequels, trilogies,
remakes,

entire cinematic universes,
to escape their own.

COLLECTOR'S ITEMS

They lined the shelves,
these tiny icons of childhood
from which I constructed stories.

I moved their joints and swiveling
features to fashion scenes
after the films I had seen, the books
I had read,

until the day came when wielding
plastic no longer made sense.
No one else my age still played
with toys.

So I put the toys away and started
playing with words.
I collect them in journals, often
the first part of a process: words I like,
words that sound interesting.

Bits of material that can be formed
together like clay with other bits.

Autographing

> Please make it out to...
> And say...

I once collected names,
but never had the experience
of a face-to-face encounter.

I probably would have disappeared
into the burbles of fandom,
barely making a sensible word.

But I found my name in those signatures
in the days before I realized
secretaries made most of the loops,

And where secretaries were busy
machines and photo copies often did
the trick.

JD DeHart

Voices Singing

When did the sounds
stop piping through?
When did music stop making sense?

It's hard to know and this chart
only shows the loss of hearing,
but not the story

(charts never elaborate too much).

Was I muted slightly, then more
and more until you thought:
>   Why does he move his mouth
>   with no real noise?

Or was the music always just noise?

WHAT DID YOU FIND?

A spyglass, the perfect chair,
a spot of room in the corner,
your favorite brush,

a memory of a room you have
never really been in, finding
your mind playing the curious
game of déjà vu,

the girl you almost kissed
in the sand of a summer long
ago but were too timid
to follow through with motion,

the question you almost asked
that would have distinguished you
from the herd
before plummeting off into the rapid
stream of seasons.

In Honor of Satire

A flash of life
reversed, shown through a funhouse
mirror, bad news brought to you
on the lips of a smiling jester.

A rhyme and a jingle
for your viewing pleasure.

A line of reportage
drawn through the writer's room
with a few twinkling jokes strung
on like Christmas lights.

Complete with an impersonator
and singer
so that the image settles well
on the stomach.Ballistic

CONFESSION

Ping was the sound
of death whizzing by, how
strange that eternity could be born
on such a small object in the wind.

A little to the left or right, and who
knows? I might not be here to recite
this poem.

How life balances delicately,
barely there, then gone, a wisp

passing by as swiftly
as that tiny bit of metal, birthed
from a blossom of erupting sound.

JD DeHart

Pretending to be Profound

By the light that streams
in, you can see through
the discourse, held up to
the light like a small animal.

Within that envelope of syntax
and highbrow terminology,

swallowing word after word,
a flurry of sound and thunder
with no lightning heat or music.

MEANS THE WORLD

I'm not sure where
the world stands anymore,
old beliefs have fallen
like slate sliding into boiling,
tense ocean.

I'm not two weeks ago me.

I'm not sure what the heavens
make of this, if they look at all,
not sure what the numbers mean
anymore, those measures of life,
collected in graphs and figures.

It used to be I looked for signs
and I wanted to read into
every action and whim of space,

wished for them to offer advice.

But now I just wonder,
just want to believe,
and wonder some more still.

JD DeHart

Thank You, Dear Author

for the signature scrawled,
for the kind words. For showing
how graceful grace can be.
Even taking the time to get to know
us a bit in a long line.

For never meeting a stranger,
for giving words to dark places
of loneliness and isolation.
For always giving words.

For reminding us of home,
of that southern twang we knew
and loved. For never letting
us forget that an ego has no place.

This is real life, these are real
hands. Splinters and tears are real,
not just what work well in a story.

THE TWINE FORT

I cordoned off a
bit of childhood in the woods
there. Just over the hill.

In my mind, it was a massive
collaboration of effort and might.
But the twine kept slipping,
much to my chagrin.

My imagination filled
in the details of the war, of the other
side, invisible, of where the vulnerable
places might be.

When I was not a superhero, I was a soldier,
when I was not a soldier, I was a teacher.
Only one of these came true.

BIRD'S NEST

There is a bird's nest
in the window, and it has been
formed of stray hair.
What birds are these?
I do not own a guidebook, and it's
times like this I almost wish I did.

Creatures collect wrappers
and human leftovers wherever they
can, and form a home. Some birds
choke on this matter, like gulls.
That's what I'm told.

A bird's nest is fine with me.

The sight of little bald heads, leathery
necks, cartoonish beaks, is a happy one,
much more so than say a rat's nest
or the dry, gray husk of hornets' home.

Packaged Neatly

We are ministers of organization,
the two of us.
And what I don't analyze is analyzed
by another.
What I don't list is listed later
in different handwriting.

Our world moves in a swift orbit.
When the table is cluttered, we can
barely focus. So, we clean it.
Objects each have a place.
Some places are ordained by basic
ontology (a mixer goes in the kitchen,
you see). Others are assigned by us.
Gloves surely go in *this* drawer.

The last two years have taught me
how we organize together, how we knit
one hand to the other's. How we
complement with words and without.

Boat Ride

Why is he afraid?
Fear really has no logical utility.
It is the mark of a higher function.

This is a simple boat ride. We have
done this a million times. Get in,
get out, move on.
Splash, splash.

And what fear is now
set up in me, seeing the pale
face and white knuckles?
Has that fear found a hollow place
in my chest and set up residence?

Is that same reluctance visited
upon me in my own shrinking?
Does it tether me back
at the shoulder?

Do I cling to corners and grab
rails for fear I will go floating
off into oblivion for this reason?

On account of my fear, alone?

Did I Ever Tell You

about the time
we discovered the cat couldn't
hear? We sat there honking the
horn, and she wouldn't move?

Nicknamed her Crazy.

And do you remember how
she climbed that tree to get
rid of those dogs, because
roaming dogs were not uncommon
in my upbringing?

Took us a long time to coax her down,
feels like hours or days in my memory
now, but who knows how long
it really was? I mean, summer seemed
to just stretch in those days.

Now, you blink and miss it, which I was
always told is how time would
go, looking back.

NEARBY

A crackle in the voice
tells me we're not so nearby
as we used to be.

Days and days of highway
stretch between us, but there is
even more,

An entire continent has formed
at the base of my neck, separating
me from the rest of the world.

I fear no land bridge will rise
here for centuries, which is an awfully
long time to be quiet.

We're not on speaking terms, I bet,
but, still, that is a cold solitude,
even when I know exchanged pleasantries
will be blistering.

THE MONTHS

The months came by to visit,
June with her sunny disposition
and April with her warming charm.
December was silent and deadly,
as usual.
August was barely dressed,
and October wore his favorite
costume, munching on candy.
The evening came, and they swept
away to set the rest of the year's
gradual time.

JD DeHart

CITATIONS SPEAK LOUDER THAN WORDS

We learn from the eminent professor
That we have nothing to say in research
That someone else has not already said.
Nothing to mention that is disconnected
From multiple spider web points of study.

We take our ideas and tie them to others.
Supporting them on the vertebrae
Of other researchers and bibliographies,
Giving them weight, spirit, and intestines,
All in MLA format, or else APA.
Birthing them to full statistical existence.

Path of Stone

What was dirt became
stone but could not pass
for pavement.

My father paved the road
with bits of gravel.
I remember him working
on it all year long.

How many stones sunk
into the earth just so our tires
could go to town, I'll
never know. No use counting
now, no stones to remove
the rumble and bump.

TONY'S CALL

came late in the evening,
I barely remember his voice.
I don't remember his last name.

What are friends to men?
I see gatherings of men. Are
they friends?

I do not speak their language
of athletes and ball stats.
I know how to talk about (some)
books and ideas.
Preferring much more to recount
the events of a film, or its strange
backstory of switching directors,
of chosen shots.

I don't remember how long we
talked, but I remember dialing
the old rotary, wondering what
we could have in common.

SALAMANDER DIP

we called it,
a slab of smooth stone someone
had hewn out of the mountain.

Care for a drink?

I watched the old man ladle
out a portion of unnaturally
cold water (or it is naturally?)
into his searching lips.
The water dripped down the grey flecks
of his beard, grey
like mine is now, but I refused
the drink, though thirsty.

Seeing a leaf inside, moving,
thinking what salamander or other
creature might have laid eggs
beneath it.

Stork

"Where do babies come from?"
the well-meaning child asks.
So the pedagogue responds:
"Once your parents loved each
other very much, although
time changes all arrangements,
and they ventured to a garden
together, meeting a stork.
The stork demanded of them
a great trial
(a bank heist or assassination
being the most common
themes at his command),
which they gladly performed.
So, dear children, in order
to get here today,
your parents loved you very
very much...but were also forced
to perform a terrible act."
When the tears have subsided,
the pedagogue tells them
there is a second, messier
way that babies are born,
but the bell rings too soon.

SADIE AND SAWYER

At the sound of their master's carburetor,
Sadie and Sawyer snuck out of their crate.

As the old owner puttered to an office,
The two small terriers sealed their fate.

There was a small hole in the back door
Through which the yapping duo could go.

Between both, with all eight legs sprinting,
They sniffed frantically for friend or foe.

Nose to the ground, they made their way,
Sadie and Sawyer, the bravest fur pair.

The sound of larger dogs bellow-barking
Did not seem to weigh them with care.

This was how the day was spent, seeking
Some grave peril or dangerous situation

For an adventure, the two of them yearned
Until the day waned and master returned.

TEREBINTH

Isaiah wrote about the stump
Left behind in the world
After the sweep of judgment fell,
The oak and the terebinth remain.

The sawed tree leaves a pattern,
Ridges and narrow passageways.
You could trace a star with
Its end, a raw, gnarled appendage.

Isaiah wrote about the ravaged
Field and ruin, which were juxtaposed
With the remainders, the seed.

The excerpt implies a peace
Larger than truth, that even when
Broken and crumbling, twisted,
There is a small grain of hope.

It lies beneath the surface, a small
Inclination of a behemoth below.

Blessing is a small, wordless child
Sitting amid the curses and fears.

MEETING OLD FRIENDS

She said,
"I'm just meeting old friends here."
But the friends never came,
never showed up for us to see.

As she baptized her corn muffin
over and over again in the steaming
soup (that stopped steaming
after a long while),

we noted they never came.
So, they must have been the ghosts
unseen, wind moving through
curtains or in unseen places,

All coming to visit her again
and again.

Previously Published Works

A Jo Bell Poem – first published at Record Magazine

An Evening in the Country – first published at Beakful

Beheaded Sheep Figurine – first published at Red River Review

Caught – first published at Synchronized Chaos

Citations Speak Louder Than Words – first published at Literary Yard

Custodian to the Young – first published at Social Justice Poetry

Frog – first published at Leaves of Ink

Grandfather – first published at Montucky Review

Gutter Mystery – first published at Beakful

Here is a Simple Test – first published at Synchronized Chaos

Heroes Need Fiction – first published at Medusa's Kitchen

John Ramm – first published at Eunoia Review

John Ramm's Retirement Party – first published at Poems and Poetry Blog

Learning How to Use a Sword – first published at Medusa's Kitchen

Means the World – first published at Literary Yard

Nabokovian – first published at Literary Yard

Narrative Creature – first published at Record Magazine

Operator – first published at Referential Magazine

Polar – first published at Leaves of Ink

Pretending to be Profound – first published at Literary Yard

Requiem for a Neighbor – first published at Literary Yard

Sadie and Sawyer – first published at Stinkwaves Magazine

Sailing – first published at Record Magazine
Sand Castle – first published at Spirit Fire Review
Stork – first published at Poet Community
Symbolism Takes a Seat – first published at Eunoia Review
Terebinth – first published at Poetry Bulawayo
The Months – first published at Poetry Bulawayo
We Caged the Minotaur – first published at Red River Review

ABOUT THE AUTHOR

JD DeHart is a writer and teacher. He is currently working on his PhD in Literacy Studies. DeHart has previously published a series of science fiction-inspired poetry, The Truth About Snails, and has published poetry, articles, and stories in a wide variety of venues.

www.ingramcontent.com/pod-product-compliance
Lightning Source LLC
Chambersburg PA
CBHW020949030426
42339CB00004B/22